A SPIRIT DAUGHTER WORKBOOK

---

written by
Jill Wintersteen

FOR THE FULL MOON

Monday, March 9th

10:47AM PDT

WHY THE FULL MOON

While the New Moon is the time we state our intentions to the Universe, the Full Moon is the time to do the work needed to manifest them. This Lunar phase is ripe with energy waiting to be harnessed, directed, and utilized to create our dreams. At this point, two weeks since the New Moon, initial blocks, or barriers may have popped up in your life, causing you to doubt your dreams. You may have even forgotten your intentions and returned back to the comfort and safety of day to day life. You may be feeling a bit lost and unsure of what steps need to be taken to bring your visions into reality. These emotions are all normal and are part of the process of creating your best life. The Full Moon is a time to return to your intentions planted on the New Moon and feel into what needs to be done to make them a reality.

Dreams take work, most of which comes in the form of energetic work on ourselves. Often it is not our circumstances that need to be adjusted, it is our own energetic vibration and the frequency we are emitting out into the Universe. The Full Moon helps make that work more apparent and illuminates the next steps we need to take. It's a time to recommit to ourselves and understand that with patience, compassion, and commitment, anything is possible. We have the opportunity each month to let go of energies that do not serve our dreams and integrate new ones that do. It is a magical time when we can feel our true potential, and use the extra energetic charge from the cosmos to pursue that potential.

Each Full Moon is positioned opposite the Sun in our skies. This opposition creates a vibration felt by us and all beings on Earth. Even animals feel the energy of a Full Moon, evident by wolves howling at it and even fish feeding more than usual during this time. The opposition of the Moon and Sun means that their gravitational pull is affecting the Earth on opposite sides, making us feel as though we are being pulled into two directions. It's no wonder the very word "lunatic" was created because of behaviors observed on and around, the Full Moon. Science has yet to define precisely why the Full Moon affects so many of us. Still, observation will tell us it has something to do with light codes, gravitational pull, and energetic vibrations of the stars in which the Moon and Sun are positioned.

The constellations comprising our zodiac each carry their own frequency, which rains down on us. These frequencies are amplified by the Sun, the Moon, and all the planets. When the Moon or Sun are within a certain sign, that astrological energy flavors the Moon phase or Sun Season. Every astrological energy has qualities or traits associated with it. On a Full Moon, the Moon and Sun are in opposing astrological energies. This opposition only adds to the friction of a Full Moon. Often we can feel the crisis between the two signs, and their qualities, in our emotional body. Each astrological energy, and every energy on the planet, has a low frequency and a high frequency. Energies like love, compassion, and forgiveness are higher energies, while frequencies like guilt, resentment, and anger are lower vibrations. Each zodiac sign has its own lows and its own highs.

During a Full Moon, all sides of each sign involved are illuminated within us. Meaning, we can see which corresponding qualities we embody within our own energetic field. Much of this illumination is what causes us to feel emotionally charged on a Full Moon. It brings our shadows into the light, revealing them, so we have no choice but to face our demons. Confronting our shadows can feel difficult and emotionally intense. It can stir up fear and even resistance. Hard work, though, is often required for growth. Our shadows are where blocks, old programming, and limiting beliefs interact, preventing us from attracting our dreams. It is where we need to send compassion, love, and forgiveness to help shift into a higher vibration. This shadow work is the topic of every Full Moon Workbook and is the key to manifesting the life of your dreams.

VIRGO FULL MOON

The Virgo Full Moon is an invitation to love yourself fully, including your imperfections, your so-called negative traits, and any lower vibrations you may carry. It is a time to become honest about who you are and accept yourself on all levels. This radical self-acceptance is exactly what gives you the power to grow and to become the best version of yourself. In this acceptance, you can let go of any illusions of perfectionism, accept that you'll never be perfect, and love yourself anyway. It is only through honoring your imperfections that you can fully love and honor your whole self. Looking at what you consider to be your flaws can be challenging, but with the help of Virgo on this Full Moon, you can learn to love every bit of yourself knowing it's your imperfections that make you unique and often give you power. They also show you where you can learn, where you can grow, and where you can vibrate higher. As we work with this Full Moon energy, know that any emotions or experiences are all happening for you to love and accept yourself more fully. Full Moons stir up many energies and can feel intense with their sleepless nights and tearful mornings, but the silver lining of this Full Moon is a chance to strengthen your relationship with yourself.

Virgo is the sign of the Goddess, she reminds us that we are more powerful than we can ever imagine. We have the ability to shape our world and claim our destiny. We choose who, and what, is allowed in our space. We are the makers of our reality, and we are the most important person in that reality. When Virgo meets the Full Moon, it's a time to feel our inherent power to define our life. It's also a time to hear our intuition. Virgo is a highly feminine sign and brings our inner knowing to the surface. Often the next steps and plans of action come effortlessly from this place. When you listen to your intuition, you are also teaching yourself to love a piece of yourself, which is often overlooked. Virgo wants you to honor your whole self, this includes your a-ha moments, flashes of insight, and intuitive hunches. When you honor your intuitive sense, you strengthen your love for yourself.

The Virgo Full Moon is also a time to define your boundaries. Virgo brings us the energy of definition and refinement. She teaches us that boundaries, when properly created, become containers for us to flourish. They help us organize our world, and they provide direction on where to place our energy. This Full Moon is a time to create boundaries with yourself, the people in your life, your time, and your space. Virgo reminds us that boundaries become easier to uphold when you love and respect yourself. Self-love is the foundation of any boundary you set in your life, including, and especially, the ones with yourself. Notice what this Full Moon reveals around your boundaries. Look at how you define your time, how you honor your commitments, and how you protect your sacred spaces. Boundaries come in many forms. They can look like appointments on your calendar for self-care, they may be five minutes of daily meditation, they may be set time slots to work on meaningful projects, and they can be guidelines on how you want to be treated by others. It's important to remember that when boundaries are violated frustration and anger arises. If you are experiencing either of these emotions, look to your boundaries for guidance on how to settle any agitation. Boundaries are a lifelong process, start to define them this Full Moon and know that they need constant upkeep, but they serve a vital part of your evolution. Without boundaries, life lacks definition, and you can end up adrift at sea, wondering how to use your infinite power.

When you have healthy boundaries, it becomes easier to vibrate higher and recognize your gifts. We each have a unique gift. Our work this lifetime is to embrace it, accept it and give it to the world. The challenge comes when we don't think our gift is good enough to share with others. The Virgo Full Moon is a time to accept that you, and your talent, are good enough. You are unique, and you are an important piece of the greater collective. When you love yourself fully, it becomes less challenging to share your gifts with the world and create a fulfilling life aligned with your purpose. It starts, though, with knowing that while you may never be perfect, you are still worthy of love, recognition, and compassion from yourself and others. Your gift does not need to perfect to be helpful or needed. It's your time to share your brilliance with the world.

VIRGO MOON X PISCES SUN

While the Moon sits in the energy of Virgo, the Sun sits in opposition with the energy of Pisces. Virgo and Pisces form a spectrum of energy where at either end exists their extremes and in the middle, where their energies meet, exists a beautiful integration of their highest vibrations. Every energy has a high side and low side. We can align with either side at any time, and we can shift from a lower vibration to a higher one with the right focus and intention. Every Full Moon brings us the opportunity to first realize if we are aligning with a lower vibration of the sign involved, then shift into a higher vibration through release work and often forgiveness. On this Virgo Full Moon, we have the support of the cosmos in stepping away from the lower vibrations of Virgo and Pisces to align with their high sides instead. Furthermore, we can merge their higher vibrations to form a fully integrated energy, which is stronger than their individual energies alone.

Pisces and Virgo offer us two different portals to that same energy of spirituality, healing, and service. Where Pisces is formless, chaotic, and all-encompassing, Virgo is form, order, and refinement. Where Virgo is worldly, connected to the Earth, Pisces is otherworldly, connected to infinite space. Pisces sees no distinction between us and another. Pisces teaches us that we are all connected through the universal consciousness, with the Universe itself living through each one of us. Virgo's energy, however, demands we stay within the boundaries of space, time and our body. She asks us to define our energy and our world. Virgo also believes we are the Universe but inspires us to create containers, through organized practices, to help us connect with our most intuitive self using direction and intent.

Pisces encourages us to not react to emotions, but rather observe the fluctuations of energy and sensations within our body and mind. From this non-reactive state, Pisces follows the flow of the Universe trusting its every twist and turn. Pisces surrenders

VIRGO MOON X PISCES SUN

to the unknown and teaches us to be patient as we watch our life unfold. Virgo, on the other hand, acts. Virgo understands the flow of the Universe but chooses to provide it with some direction. She recognizes when boundaries are needed between us and other people. Virgo reminds us that while trust and surrender are important, so are direction and guidance. The Universe will respond to deadlines and time limits if we state them. We can have boundaries even with the Universe. We do not have to sit around patiently forever, waiting for our dreams to manifest. Virgo teaches us that we can make some reasonable demands. We can ask, for example, to see a sign in the next six months, or to have a dream come into fruition within in a year. Our job then becomes to trust that what doesn't unfold on our timeline may be an opportunity for redirection.

As Pisces and Virgo's energies dance with each other this Full Moon, their lower vibrations are also revealed. The low or shadow side of Pisces includes escapism, addiction, and co-dependency. These conditions stem from the lack of boundaries between Pisces and the outside world, causing too many emotions. When we align with this side of Pisces, we take on a myriad of external energies. We become unaware of which emotions are our own and which ones belong to someone else. We then seek behaviors that help us drown out all feelings, so we do not have to sort through them, but rather escape them. The other side of this escapism is to get lost in empathy and feel everything to the point of losing touch with oneself through full enmeshment with the energies of others. These extreme sides of Pisces cause us to forget our boundaries, our sense of self, and our true feelings.

Virgo, on the other hand, can be too confining. The low vibrations of this sign are perfectionism, overbearing behavior, and extreme detail to spatial configurations. The extreme low side of Virgo is rigidity and over-analysis to the point of paralysis. When we align with the lower vibrations of Virgo, we procrastinate from fear of failure, we suffer from anxiety over inconsequential mistakes, and we waste time going over projects needlessly. We also focus too much on time. We never feel we have enough of it, and we waste time merely worrying about it.

Without judgment and with compassion, begin to think about ways in which you may exhibit either of these lower vibratory states. As you bring your awareness to the lower vibrations of Pisces and Virgo, you open the door to shift them into a higher state. Awareness is the first step for release. As you shift the lower vibrations, you can fully integrate the higher vibrations of Pisces and Virgo. This leads to a non-reactive self who is in full control of their inner and outer worlds. A person who loves and accepts themselves fully, knowing they are part of the vast Universe. This connection brings forth endless inner knowledge and imagination. When aligned with both Pisces and Virgo, it becomes easy to create flexible boundaries, which provide direction to your life. They allow you to go with the flow, but also provide some direction to the current without controlling it.

Furthermore, when aligned with the high sides of both Pisces and Virgo, you can see the potential in everything but stay detached from the outcome. You can see the perfect version without having to obtain it, but instead using it for inspiration. Rather than creating expectations and demands of yourself, you can love yourself fully. In that love, you can heal any broken pieces which need compassion, not avoidance, without feeling pressure to put yourself back together. You can love yourself for who you are today, as is, one who is perfectly imperfect.

VIRGO ASPECTS

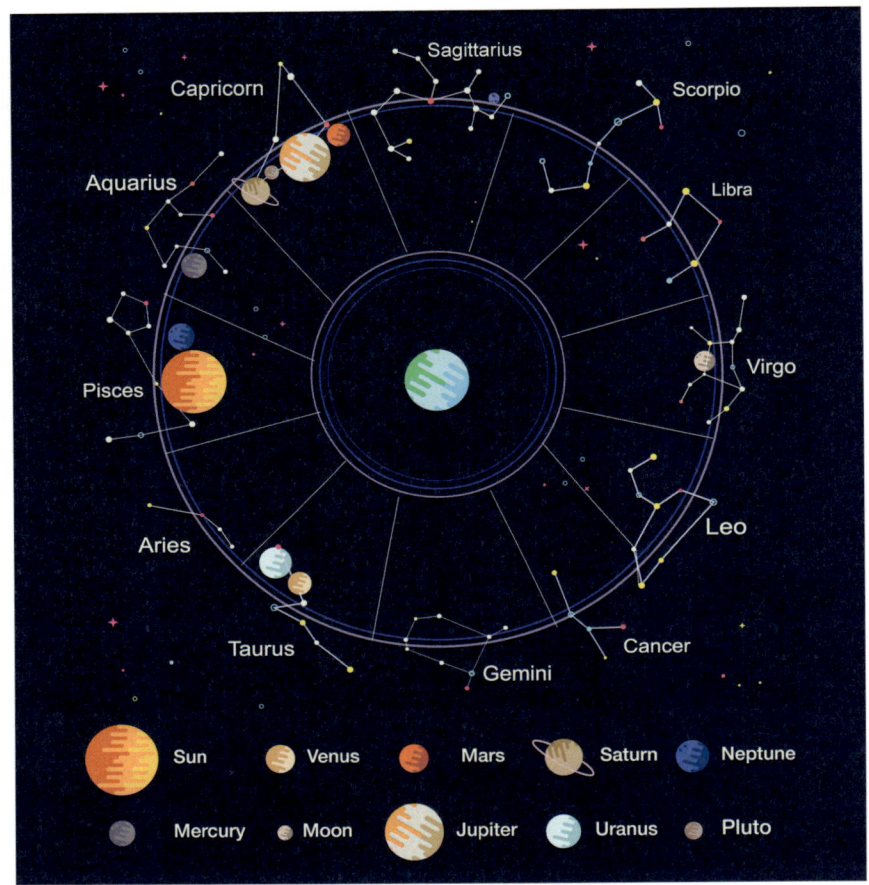

The main aspect of this Full Moon is the opposition of the Sun and Moon, but there are many other influences and energies to work with on this day. Almost every planet, except Saturn, is involved in this Full Moon. Additionally, all planets, except Mercury, are in feminine astrological signs, with the majority of them sitting in Earth signs. Overall, this is a high energetically charged Full Moon brimming with feminine Earth energy. When we look at each piece of this Full Moon puzzle, we find many additional energies guiding us this day and helping us harness her magic.

The first influence of the day is Mercury stationing direct. Mercury has been retrograde since February 16th, and at 8:48 PM PST, it turns direct. Mercury is the planetary ruler of Virgo, and this transit has a significant impact on the Full Moon. When Mercury leaves retrograde motion, it energetically feels like a slingshot, especially in the realm of our communication. Our speech and other methods of communicating become unblocked, and much like a cork popping out of a champagne bottle, words can fly. Be aware of oversharing information on this Full Moon, as well as saying things you may not have thought about first. If you find yourself overexcited when speaking or even rambling, connect with the Earth to ground you and your communication. Take deep breaths and recenter your thoughts before continuing in your conversation. Also, ground yourself before completing the practices in this workbook, so your mind is clear as you communicate with yourself.

VIRGO ASPECTS

Neptune also plays a big role this Full Moon. The Sun, in Pisces, is sitting next to Neptune as they both oppose the Moon in Virgo. Neptune is the planet of dreams. It helps us tap into our imagination and visions. Neptune also reminds us to look at any illusions we may have and differentiate between what feels like a fantasy and what feels possible. We have the power to manifest any dream, but if we don't believe it can happen, then our power vanishes. If an affirmation or intention feels like a fantasy, then our energy will find it hard to accept it and project it into the world. On this Full Moon, allow Neptune to help you create visions and affirmations which feel possible to you. This does not mean they are small or limit you in any way, it just means that every part of you believes in them and your potential to create them.

Our next players this Full Moon are; Mars, Jupiter, and Pluto, all sitting next to each other in Capricorn. Saturn is also sitting in Capricorn but is a little out of reach to influence this Full Moon. Mars, Jupiter, and Pluto are within range, though, as they sextile, or form a 60° angle, with the Sun in Pisces and trine, or form 120° angle, with the Moon in Virgo.

Mars is the planet of passion, lust, and war. It brings a fiery energy to this Full Moon. In Capricorn, Mars' energy is more grounded than usual, but it still adds an element of passion, which can also bring an element of agitation. Mars reminds us that when our boundaries are crossed, we often feel angered or resentful. This includes boundaries with ourselves, the most important of all the ones we set. As you work with setting limits, both with yourself and others, feel if any of the boundaries already feel infringed upon or are triggering you in some way. Remember that Mars is working with us this Full Moon. Sextile and trines are beneficial aspects. Mars is helping you to understand your boundaries, although sometimes this process can feel irritating. If frustrations arise, connect with the Earth to cool you and ask yourself what is at the heart of your frustration?

Jupiter is the planet of expansion, luck, and faith. It lends its energy this Full Moon by reminding us that we have more potential than we could ever imagine. Jupiter in Capricorn turns our attention to where we may be selling ourselves short and not giving ourselves a chance to shine. On this Full Moon, look at how your need for perfection, or any feelings of unworthiness, may be blocking your potential. Take a leap and accept the outcome even if it's imperfect or doesn't meet your expectations. Know that what unfolds is precisely what is meant to be for you at this point in your journey.

Pluto reminds us of the ongoing cycles of our energy. It is the planet of rebirth and teaches us that our energy is infinite throughout time and space. What we do today impacts tomorrow and our next life. Furthermore, many of the wounds which need healing are leftover from past lives and have resurfaced tp receive love and compassion this life. With Pluto influencing this Full Moon, it becomes a time to love and accept your past. It's a time to honor where you have been and heal any traumas that remain. Pluto teaches us that everything we experience is part of a larger unfolding of our energy. We may not understand it yet, but our life is a beautifully orchestrated dance of entangled energy. On this Full Moon, heal yourself through the acceptance of your journey and honor the strength of the person you are today.

The other planets involved on this Full Moon are Venus and Uranus in Taurus. While they are not directly aspecting the Moon, their conjunction creates an intense energy that influences the overall vibrations of this week. Venus is the feminine planet of love and beauty, and Uranus is the planet of change and progress. Together in Taurus, they inspire us to honor our intuition and use it to create a new way of life. This conjunction reminds us of the power of femininity and asks us how we can redefine what that means to us and the world. In combination with the Virgo Full Moon, these energies help us feel our inner Goddess, gender aside, and her power. Feel your strength and know it comes from a place of receptivity and softness versus a place of action and force. Also, feel your inner knowing and ask to be guided this Full Moon in finding the inspiration you need to create the changes you want to see in your life.

HOUSESCOPES

First House in Virgo

The first house governs our identity, our appearance, and the energy we project outwardly to the world. With Virgo here, you pride yourself on being seen as an organized, detail-oriented person who arrives on time eager to greet any challenge. You also tend to hide your imperfections from the world, only allowing others to see the unflawed side of you. As the Full Moon transits your first house, allow it to illuminate parts of yourself that usually do not see the light of day. Challenge yourself to accept your imperfections and share them with those closest to you, then share them with the world. Let this Full Moon show you that your flaws are what make you perfect, special, and unique. They are a gift.

Second House in Virgo

The second house governs our resources, our possessions, and our self-worth. With Virgo here, you tend to place great value on your attention to detail and your ability to analyze any situation. You tend to put pressure on yourself to be perfect and can find it challenging to feel worthy when you feel flawed. You live by the assumption that abundance is only granted to those who work hard, are dedicated, and deserve it. With the Full Moon transiting your second house, expect issues around resources, abundance, and finances to arise. Challenge yourself to believe that you are worthy of great wealth and abundance in all areas with less effort than what you have told yourself is required.

Third House in Virgo

The third house governs our communication and how we exchange energy with the world. With Virgo here, your conversations tend to be clear, concise, and well organized. You are meticulous in your speech and tend to expect others to be the same. With the Full Moon transiting this house, you may feel the need to speak up more now than ever before. Watch that your words don't come out too fast and remember to use your intelligent mind before you speak. If you do say something you regret, align with the releasing aspect of this Full Moon to forgive yourself.

Fourth House in Virgo

The fourth house governs our home, our subjective thoughts, and our most intimate emotions. With Virgo governing this house, the challenge becomes to love yourself and all of your feelings. You are not something that needs to be fixed or hidden, but rather a being in need of love, acceptance, and compassion. With the Full Moon transiting this house, love all the pieces of yourself, even the ones which feel broken. Challenge yourself to shine light on your scars and heal the deepest parts of your soul with the strength of your love.

Fifth House in Virgo

The fifth house governs our play and how we embrace joy in our world. With Virgo here, the challenge becomes letting go of the details long enough to have some fun. You tend to criticize your creativity and forget that some of the most beautiful creations are messy, chaotic, and unorganized. With the Full Moon transiting this house, challenge yourself to let go of any need to be perfect and just feel free. Allow yourself to create freely and align with your heart's joy, without criticism, judgment, or analysis. Embrace chaos in your world and find happiness in the mess.

Sixth House in Virgo

The sixth house governs service and is the natural home of Virgo. Virgo and the sixth house are not equal, but share many things in common. With Virgo in your sixth house, you tend to feel fulfilled when helping others and take great pride in your ability to see things others cannot. You are a wonderful healer and use your attention to detail to find solutions to issues that can feel overwhelming to other people. Allow this Full Moon to illuminate your most intuitive side and rest your practical side, which you often rely upon. Feel the beauty of your inner knowledge and allow it to show you the way to your next steps.

*You can look up your houses at astro-charts.com

HOUSESCOPES

Seventh House in Virgo

The seventh house governs our relationships and partnerships. With Virgo here, you bring detail and attention to your relationships. You also bring intellect. You inspire your partners to focus, create clear visions, and follow your lead. You tend to choose partners who are grounded and thrive in relationships that bring you down to earth. With the Full Moon transiting your seventh house, expect the spotlight to be on your relationships. Focus on the ones which help you love and accept yourself and begin to shift any which feel overly critical or reflect your own need for perfection.

Eighth House in Virgo

The eighth house governs personal growth and transformation. With Virgo here, you are on a quest to heal deep wounds, possibly from another life. You understand the importance of your intuition and use it to help resolve conditioned patterns. It can be helpful for you to schedule times to focus solely on your growth when the rest of the world fades into the distance of your consciousness. With the Full Moon transiting your eighth house, it becomes a time for you to focus on what in your life needs transformation. Focus on full acceptance of yourself, including your wounds, to help you evolve into your next version.

Ninth House in Virgo

The ninth house governs truth and knowledge, including the exploration of different cultures through travel. With Virgo here, you approach new experiences with an analytical mind, studying each piece as you digest it for information. You can find it challenging to get lost in the wonder of travel, relying primarily on your logic instead of your strong intuition. As the Full Moon transits your ninth house, challenge yourself to become immersed in an experience. Instead of looking at it from every angle, notice how it makes you feel, what it inspires within you, and how it helps you connect to your heart.

Tenth House in Virgo

The tenth house governs our career and how we show up in the world. With Virgo here, you tend to choose work that utilizes your sharp mind and keen intellect. You are detail-oriented in everything you do and excel at careers that make use of your analytical mind. You tend to be a perfectionist and could find it helpful to allow yourself to be imperfect at times. As the Full Moon transits your tenth house, challenge yourself to see your flaws, and accept them as part of your beauty. Release the need to be seen as perfect by the people in your life and know that your work will still be honored and valued even if you make a mistake or two.

Eleventh House in Virgo

The eleventh house governs our friends and acquaintances. With Virgo here, you love to help the people in your life. You enjoy being of service and need healthy boundaries to protect your energy. You are a natural healer and extend your skills to others, guiding them through their process of healing. As the Full Moon transits your eleventh house, honor the work you do in healing those around you. Accept your natural gifts and even refine them, bringing them to a new level. Also, challenge yourself to look at your relationship with your boundaries. Not everyone deserves access to your energy all the time.

Twelfth House in Virgo

The twelfth house governs our spiritual growth. With Virgo here, you dive deep into the spiritual realm but in a very organized way. You tend to study spirituality, including differing philosophies, religions, alternative approaches, and varying methods of yoga and meditation. You are a student of your own spiritual growth and benefit greatly from scheduled times, including classes, which afford you space to further your explorations. As the Full Moon transits your twelfth house, feel into your intuitive, mystical side. Release your need for logical answers and accept that not all magic can be explained.

*You can look up your houses at astro-charts.com

VIRGO LUNAR FLOW

Sun Salutation A - 3x

Start standing on the top of your mat. Inhale, stretch your arms overhead. Exhale, fold forward. Inhale lengthen out your back. Exhale, step back into plank pose and lower to the ground. Inhale, reach your chest up for cobra pose, legs stay on the ground. Exhale, stretch back to Downward Dog Pose. Stay here for 5 breaths and feel your entire body expand. On Exhale, step back to the top of the mat. Inhale lengthen out through your spine. Exhale, fold forward. Inhale come up to standing, reaching arms overhead. Exhale, hands return to your heart. Pause for a moment and feel centered on the ground and centered through your body. Repeat this sequence three times.

Sun Salutation B - 3x

Stand at the top of your mat. Inhale, stretch your arms overhead and bend your knees into Chair Pose. Exhale, fold forward. Inhale, lengthen out your back. Exhale, step into plank pose and lower halfway to Chatarunga (elbows into ribs). Inhale, reach your chest up for Upward-Facing Dog, with everything off the ground except your hands and feet. Exhale, Downward Dog Pose. Inhale, step left foot forward to Warrior 1, with the back foot flat at a 45-degree angle, bend into the front knee and lift your arms to the sky, 5 breaths here. Exhale, release into plank, then lower to Chaturanga. Inhale, Upward-Facing Dog. Exhale, Downward Facing Dog. Repeat on the right side, then remain in Downward Dog for 5 breaths. Exhale, step to the top of the mat. Inhale, lengthen through your spine. Exhale, fold forward. Inhale, Chair Pose. Exhale, hands to heart, breathe at the top of your mat as you feel your energy circulating throughout your body.

Warrior 2 > Reverse Warrior > Triangle > Wide Legged Forward Bend > Goddess Pose

Step your feet about 3-4 feet apart on your mat, facing the right side of your mat, feet parallel. Turn your left foot to face the front of your mat, the right foot turns in slightly. Extend your arms out to either side and bend your left knee into Warrior 2. Breath here for 5 breaths and feel the strength of your legs supporting you. On inhale, flip your left palm up to the sky, exhale, stretch back into Reverse Warrior for 5 breaths. Elongate through your left side waist. Inhale, lift your torso back up and straighten your left leg. Exhale, extend from your torso, reaching forward and place your left hand on the ground on the outside of your left foot, or on your shin and rotate your torso to the right. Stretch and reach upwards through your right arm, feeling one long line of energy from fingertip to fingertip. Take 5 full breaths here, feeling your weight evenly on both feet. On inhale, lift your torso back up and bring your feet to parallel. Place your hands on your hips, take a deep inhale, reaching your chest up, and fold forward on your exhale. Release your hands to the ground and allow your spine and neck to fully release, feeling completely supported by your legs. Take 5 breaths here. Place your hands back on your hips and slowly come up to standing. Turn your toes out to a 45-degree angle and bend in your knees for Goddess Pose. Bend your arms by your side with your palms up the sky. Breathe here for 5 breaths as you feel your feet root into the ground. Straighten your legs and rotate your right foot towards the back of the mat and practice the entire sequence on the other side.

Tree Pose

Step your feet to the top of the mat, bringing them together. Slowly bring the right foot up for tree pose, placing it on the inside of the left leg. Press firmly down through your standing leg, imagining roots going down into the Earth, providing you with balance. Reach and lengthen your spine upward, growing taller through your torso as you lift your arms to the sky. Take 5 deep breaths here before switching sides.

Chair Pose > Standing Forward Bend

Return to the front of your mat. Keep your feet together and bend deeply into your knees as if you were sitting in a chair. Reach your arms upward to the sky and look up. Feel your belly drawing in, helping to direct your tailbone to the floor. Breathe here for 5 breaths and feel the strength of your legs. Inhale, come back up to standing, exhale, fold forward for 5 breaths, allowing your torso to lengthen again. On inhale, slowly roll up to standing.

Janu Sirsansa

Place a blanket or a bolster underneath your hips for the next sequence. Extend your right leg in front of you while bending your left knee out to the side. Place your left foot at the inside of your right thigh for Janu Sirsasana. Inhale, reach your arms overhead, lengthening through your torso; exhale, fold over your right leg. Hold here for 5 breaths. On each inhale, expand your ribs and stretch your spine on each exhale fold a little deeper. Slowly come up and switch sides. Keep your mind occupied by returning to the four-count breath from the beginning.

Supine Twist

Remain on your back. Hug your left knee into your chest, twisting to the right side. You can place your bolster or block under this knee to give support to your twist. Stretch your right arm out to the side, but keep the neck neutral. Fill your low back with your air as you breathe, releasing more into the twist on each exhale. After 5 breaths, slowly come up and switch sides.

Savasana

Stretch both your legs out long on the mat and place your palms facing upward in a receptive motion. Feel your entire body supported by the ground beneath you. Let your breath become natural and feel the energy circulating through you from your practice. Allow your mind to be still and your body to be calm.

VIRGO MEDITATION

Four-Part Abdominal Breathing

The Virgo Full Moon can rattle our nervous system and make us feel on edge. This nervousness is one of Virgo's low sides and can stir up anxiety about our choices this day. It can also make us want to cling to the familiar and not go with the flow of Pisces, blocking our ability to surrender to the life we were born to live. The following meditation is a simple breathwork proven to help down-regulate your nervous system. Practice it on the day before and the day of the Full Moon to help you stay calm and able to confront all of the energies this Full Moon brings into the light.

If possible, practice this breathwork outside to connect fully with the energy of Mother Earth. Begin in a comfortable seated position, or you can practice lying down. Relax through your shoulders and your neck. Feel the full weight of your body supported by the floor or ground beneath you. Close your eyes and begin to inhale, first into your chest, then into your belly, for a count of four. The inhale will feel like a wave moving through your torso, expanding each part completely. Hold the breath for a count of four as you relax into the present moment. Exhale for a count of four, fully emptying the lungs. Finally, hold the breath out for a count of four, relaxing your body as you hold. This last part can be the hardest, notice if any fear or anxiety arises as you hold the breath out. Consciously relax around any tension, knowing you are safe and supported. This sequence is one complete round. Continue to breathe like this for five minutes, feeling your body and mind relax with each round. When finished, slowly open your eyes and allow the light to reenter. Feel yourself centered and connected to your body.

White Light Meditation

Much of the work of this Virgo Full Moon revolves around creating healthy boundaries in our life. One place you can start is energetically with this visualization meditation. Through this practice, you will encase your body and aura, with a white light. This light will help to shield you from negativity and other people's energies. Practicing this technique will make it easier to create other boundaries throughout your day. Practice on the Full Moon and any other time when you feel the need to create a buffer between yourself and the world.

Practice this meditation in a comfortable seated position, feeling yourself rooted into the ground. Close your eyes. Before beginning, breathe into any bodily tension to release it and fully relax your physical body. As you inhale, envision a white light coming up from the ground swirling around your body to the crown of your head. As you exhale, see the light fall around you, encasing your body in a white, translucent egg, forming an outer layer of protection. Continue this five times. Afterward, see the light directly above you like the Sun or a flashlight. Allow this stronger light to shine down on you, further encasing you with light, creating another layer of protection. Spend about 3-5 minutes seeing this light rain down on you. Then sit amongst your white light, feeling it allow in what you deem worthy and keep away anything you don't want in your field. As you slowly open your eyes and start to move about your day, feel this white light go with you wherever you roam. Know that it is helping to shield you and give you an energetic boundary.

CIRCLE SET UP

This grounding and defining Full Moon in Virgo occurs at the very start of Pisces Season, giving us the elements of Earth and Water. The combination of Earth and Water creates a mud, a very detoxifying substance. Consider this circle a place which can help rid yourself of energies you no longer want, while providing new inspiration directly from your most intuitive self. You can practice alone or in the company of others. If you do practice in a community, choose to be surrounded by people you are comfortable enough to speak freely with about your feelings, your process of release, and your newly formed creations.

Choose a quiet location to set up your Moon Circle, either inside or outside. Incorporate all the elements, especially Water and Earth. For Air, incorporate auric sprays, feathers to fan the smudge sticks, and even wind chimes to hear the air moving around you. Choose candles to represent Fire, or build an outside fire. You can use crystals to represent the Earth element. Crystals which align with the energy of Virgo are Smokey Quartz, Unakite, Pink Calcite, and Amazonite. These crystals will align you with your intuition while centering your energy. Also, include some crystals to represent Pisces, as this energy is very much involved tonight; crystals such as Amethyst, Aquamarine, Ocean Jasper, Angelite, and Blue Lace Agate. These crystals will help you further tap into your intuition while opening the door for trust and surrender to enter. Bring in the element of Water through a room diffuser, a vase with flowers in it, or just a simple silver metal bowl containing water. Gather all of your supplies and start to build your circle.

Create an outline with your objects, anchoring the four directions, North, South, East, and West, with either a crystal or candle. If you are creating an altar, set it up in the westerly part of the circle, as this direction gives way for the release of energies. Once the perimeter is set, cleanse the area with sage or palo santo. Begin cleansing at the Easterly point, moving to the South, West, North, then back to the East. Imagine a white light encasing the circle, protecting it from any external energies. Light your candles, and place the rest of your crystals in the circle. Place larger crystals, or a crystal grid, in the center to anchor your circle. Before your guests enter, cleanse each one of them with sage or palo santo, and then cleanse yourself. Once you have all entered the circle, pause for a moment to let the energy settle before you begin.

Follow your intuitive guidance when leading a circle. As a guide, begin with each member introducing themselves. Talk about the astrological energy of the day and how it is affecting each one of you. Share and learn from each other about your unique experiences with this Full Moon. Give plenty of space for each person to speak. Follow your conversation with the meditation practice in this book to calm the mind. You can then begin exploring the rest of the practices. Do them alone, but share as much, or as little, with the rest of the group. Go over the questions and continue to learn from each other's perspectives.

Once you're finished with the practice, spend some time in meditation again, to allow the work to integrate into your energy. Afterward, draw some cards to help tap into your own intuitive guidance. You can use any cards that you like, including Tarot, Medicine cards, or any Affirmation cards. Close the circle by giving gratitude to everyone who chose to honor the Full Moon with you. Give thanks to the elements for supporting you, and for the energy of the Universe guiding you along the way.

VIRGO CARD READING

Reading Cards is a beautiful way to access your intuition and tap into your, and the Universe's, higher wisdom. Anyone can pull cards, as long as you are willing to receive the information they provide. You need no prior experience, or training, just an open and clear mind.

You may use any cards you like for this practice, including but not limited to: Tarot Cards, Animal Medicine Cards, Oracle Cards or any Affirmation Cards. You also can pull cards from a few decks to gain different perspectives. If you are new to card pulling, try to ask only one deck the same question, as asking different decks the same question can become quite confusing. Below are some general guidelines on how to pull cards. Please improvise as needed and above anything else, listen to your intuition.

Clear your mind

A settled, grounded mind is essential for pulling cards. The last thing you want is random thoughts running around when you are trying to receive clear answers from yourself. Practice the breath work and meditation in this workbook to prepare and settle your mind. You may also clear your mind using sound frequencies through singing bowls. These can either be crystal or metal bowls. Play the bowl, or bowls, for about 3-5 minutes to help rid your mind of external noise as you focus on the harmony of the sound.

VIRGO CARD READING

Pick your deck

There are many different decks out there. You can choose as many as you like. Know, though, that they each provide you a different energy or medicine. Tarot Cards are the most popular and should be used carefully. Although very useful, Tarot cards can give the wrong impression if you interpret them harshly. Animal Medicine cards offer different types of messages from the animal realm which can help align with the spirit of nature. These cards give you the medicine you need to apply to your situation or question. Affirmation cards provide you with guidance in the form of words or phrases. When reading these cards, it is best to meditate on what the affirmation means for you. It is also helpful to repeat the affirmation a few times and see how it makes you feel. There are many other cards you can experiment with, like Goddess Cards, Angel Cards, and so on. The important thing to remember with any card is that they each have different angles and sides. There are often a few interpretations of the same card.

Shuffle

Shuffle the cards the easiest way for you. Some cards are smaller and can be shuffled like a regular deck of playing cards, while others with take some effort. If all else fails, spread them out on the floor in front of you then regather them. Keep a clear mind while shuffling. You can also repeat " I am open to receiving guidance and intuition." Refrain from asking your questions until the next step.

Virgo Card Questions

You are free to ask the deck any questions you need answers to on this Full Moon. The following questions are meant to help you harness the energy of Virgo through the cards to clarify some of these energies in your mind. This is a three-part card reading, where you'll ask the deck three questions. Before beginning, spread your freshly shuffled cards in a wide arc in front of you. Use your left middle finger to choose the card, first waving your hand slowly over the cards. You'll feel a magnetic pull, or slight tingle, in your fingertip when you hover over the right card. Chose one card at a time, taking a moment to breathe in between questions. Keep the cards flipped over until you pull all three.

1. What energy will help me release any anxiety around being perfect?

2. What energy will help me accept my imperfections?

3. What energy will help me honor my unique gifts?

Take Them In

Once you have your cards, flip them over. Before looking up their meaning, sit with them for a moment and allow them to speak to you. Intuit your own meaning and interpretation of the card. What is the card trying to tell you? What are you trying to tell yourself? After a few moments with the cards, look up their meaning. Sit with that information, merging it with your intuitive meaning of the cards.

As with everything, enjoy this process. Do not worry if you are doing it right or wrong. Just follow your intuition, and trust the journey. Accept the cards you are dealt and use their energy wisely to help guide you when you need it the most.

"Loving yourself through your fuck ups is also self-care."

- spirit daughter

VIRGO PRACTICES

The Virgo Full Moon brings us an opportunity to heal through full acceptance and love of ourselves. It is a time to honor our imperfections and acknowledge their place in our journey. This Full Moon can be a wonderful time of immense growth as it opens the door for us to love ourselves on the deepest level possible. Our challenge is to show up fully and be willing to confront all sides of ourselves, even the ones we wish to hide or avoid. This is a time of honesty and can feel emotionally intense, or even stressful, as we confront the ways we haven't loved ourselves in the past. In facing all of our imperfections, we make space for ourselves to heal, to love, and to grow. In loving our imperfections, we teach ourselves that we are always worthy and deserving of love in spite of any perceived flaws, missteps, or shortcomings.

Take some time this Full Moon to see yourself clearly, including your imperfections. Know that in accepting these parts of yourself, you open the door for great healing. You also take pressure off of yourself to be perfect, reducing your overall stress level and making your life more enjoyable. Additionally, when you can admit your imperfections to yourself, you can admit them to others. This opening allows the people in your life to see you fully and love every aspect. When we reveal our truth to others, and they accept us for it, we end up feeling more at ease with them. We trust them more, have better conversations, deeper connections, and long-lasting friendships. We also open ourselves up to receiving guidance and help. When we hide behind the mask of perfection, no one can help us because we fail to admit we need help. Once we accept our imperfections, it becomes easy to ask for guidance, when needed, to fully receive the energy another has to give.

The key to working with your imperfections is to do it with love. As we work with the energy of this Full Moon, let go of any desires to analyze or critique yourself. There is no judgment here, just deep self-acceptance of yourself. You are not looking for flaws to perfect, but rather flaws to love. You may end up resolving or shifting some imperfections just through your gentle awareness and compassion, but that is not the end goal of this Moon. You are not something that needs to be fixed. You are not a puzzle that needs to be solved, but rather a perfectly imperfect being that needs to be embraced and loved. As you view your imperfections, remember you are not trying to fix them, you are attempting to accept them. You may heal them through your acceptance, but that is a side effect, not the primary purpose.

As you work through the practices of this Full Moon, allow the answers to come from your intuition. This is a Moon ripe with intuitive power and can open the door for your inner guidance. When you move from your intuition, life effortlessly flows in the direction of your highest visions. In some ways, it can feel almost too easy because intuitive guidance comes in quickly and gives answers immediately. When using the logical mind, solutions require long hours of comparing, discerning, and analyzing. On the other hand, intuition is a flash of insight taking only seconds. This instant knowing can make us feel like it's too good to be true, as most of us are conditioned to work hard for answers. Your intuition is amazing, though, and can provide inspiration, ah-ha moments, and the answers you need in the blink of an eye. Open yourself to receiving your guidance and intuition before continuing to the practices on the next page.

VIRGO PRACTICES

1. What areas of yourself need more compassion, love, and acceptance?

VIRGO PRACTICES

2. How do you treat your imperfections? Do you avoid them, try to fix them, or accept them?

_____

_____

_____

_____

_____

_____

_____

_____

_____

_____

_____

_____

_____

_____

_____

_____

_____

_____

_____

_____

_____

_____

_____

_____

_____

_____

_____

VIRGO PRACTICES

3. What imperfections do you hide from yourself? From others?

VIRGO PRACTICES

4. Would others view your imperfections as such? Often, what we
    think is imperfect, someone else wouldn't even notice or would
    view as an asset.

_____

_____

_____

_____

_____

_____

_____

_____

_____

_____

_____

_____

_____

_____

_____

_____

_____

_____

_____

_____

_____

_____

_____

_____

_____

_____

VIRGO PRACTICES

5. How can you see your imperfections as gifts? How can you see them as part of the unique masterpiece which is you?

VIRGO PRACTICES

6. What helps you quiet your logical/analytical mind so you can hear your intuition and make it the the leader of your energy?

_____

_____

_____

_____

_____

_____

_____

_____

_____

_____

_____

_____

_____

_____

_____

_____

_____

_____

_____

_____

_____

_____

_____

_____

_____

_____

_____

_____

VIRGO PRACTICES

7. What are three things you can do this week to love yourself more?

_____

_____

_____

_____

_____

_____

_____

_____

_____

_____

_____

_____

_____

_____

_____

_____

_____

_____

_____

_____

_____

_____

_____

_____

VIRGO PRACTICES

8. When we love ourselves, creating boundaries becomes easy, especially with ourselves. Part of honoring our imperfections is creating boundaries that protect us from being overly critical or hard on ourselves. What boundaries can you create for yourself to honor your unique energy?

_____

_____

_____

_____

_____

_____

_____

_____

_____

_____

_____

_____

_____

_____

_____

_____

_____

_____

_____

_____

_____

_____

_____

VIRGO PRACTICES

9. What boundaries do you need to create with other people which reflect your love for yourself?

VIRGO PRACTICES

10. How can you create these boundaries from love versus resentment or anger? When we create boundaries from love, they become easier to state and easier to uphold. They also have more of an impact because they carry the vibration of love.

_____

_____

_____

_____

_____

_____

_____

_____

_____

_____

_____

_____

_____

_____

_____

_____

_____

_____

_____

_____

_____

_____

_____

LAST QUARTER

MARCH 16TH | SAGITTARIUS

Last Quarter Moons occur when the Moon squares the Sun or is exactly 90 degrees away from it. This angle is what creates our Half Moon. Square aspects feel like friction in our lives. The Last Quarter Square illuminates energy, which is holding us back, bringing it to the forefront of our consciousness. This tension we feel is often within the interacting energies of the Moon and the Sun sign. The opportunity of every square is to break through the pressure and create a higher vibration between the energies involved.

Sagittarius is the energy of adventure. She inspires us to take leaps of faith and rewrite our truths. Sagittarius is always in search of new knowledge, which will help her create new stories of the world around her. She travels far and wide for this knowledge and inspires us to search within ourselves for new ways of thinking and new perspectives.

During the Sagittarius, Last Quarter, challenge yourself to let go of stories that prevent you from healing. Much of Pisces season is focused on healing and learning how to go with the flow of your life. Allow Sagittarius to show you new perspectives that will rewrite old stories of pain and suffering that block you from your higher guidance. Rid yourself of any truths which are not yours or no longer apply to your life. As you detach from these things, you'll feel your energy merge with the universal knowledge and drop into the rhythm of your life.

Also, on this Last Quarter, decide what may be preventing you from taking a leap of faith. This may be fear of the unknown, mistrust of the universe, or attachments to comfort zones. Let go of whatever is holding you back from stepping into a new life and trusting that you will always be taken care of by yourself and the universe. Trust your intuition, and let anything that goes against it be sent away with the diminishing light of the Moon.

What are you willing to let go this Last Quarter Moon to allow yourself to receive new energy?

AFFIRMATIONS

Write 3-5 old programs, or mantras, which reflect any fears, unaccpetance of yourself or lack of self-love. Know as you write them, you are releasing them.

Write 3-5 mantras which stem from complete love and acceptance of yourself. Any time your old programs pop up, meet them with your new mantras. Do this as many times as needed to shift your old habits. Repetition is the best way to reprogram yourself.

HAPPY FULL MOON

Thank you to everyone who supported and purchased this workbook.

Special Thanks to Rebecca Reitz (rebeccareitz.com, IG:@becca_reitz) for her beautiful artwork on the cover and pages 2, 4, 6, 14, 32.

For a monthly subscription contact hello@spiritdaughter.com or visit www.spiritdaughter.com